South Central Elementary L
Union Mills, Indiana

S0-AFM-997

Inspiring Quotes

Inspiring Quotes

200

Sayings

and

Poems

leonard roy frank

Gramercy Books
New York

This 2005 edition is published by Gramercy Books, an imprint of Random House Value Publishing, by arrangement with Random House Reference, divisions of Random House, Inc., New York.

Gramercy is a registered trademark and the colophon is a trademark of Random House, Inc.

Random House
New York • Toronto • London • Sydney • Auckland
www.randomhouse.com

Printed and bound in China.

A catalog record for this title is available from the Library of Congress.

ISBN 0-517-22553-0

10 9 8 7 6 5 4 3 2 1

INTRODUCTION

*F*or many of us, life consists of long stretches of boredom interspersed with moments of joy and misery; hopefully, a lot more of the former than the latter. But life can be difficult. The humdrumness of dailiness can disintegrate into one rotten thing after another, and in both the personal and political worlds, one crisis after another. With few let-ups and the pressure building, doubts crowd the mind. We question our core beliefs and begin to worry about the well-being of ourselves, the people we love and care about, and the community at large. We look out on a half-lit sky and wonder: is it night's prelude or the dawning of a new day? It is especially at such times that we search our hearts and memories and available external resources for the words of encouragement and hope that will enable us to carry on.

Assembled in these pages are more than 180 inspirational thoughts that I've found useful at critical junctures in my own life. That they worked for me doesn't mean that they'll necessarily work for the reader, but, at the least, they can provide a foundation on which any reader can build his or her own structure of inspirational wisdom. Here are quotes of sages from various cultures and times, including the Bible. Included, too, are a number of proverbs, or people's wisdom, whose authors are unknown but whose influence is widespread.

There is, of course, no way to sum up the message of a book such as this, but if I had to give it a try, I would say this: There must be some exalted purpose, at best imperfectly understood but capable of realization, that will justify the terrible suffering that human and animal life has had to endure on this planet.

Inspiring Quotes

*E*VERY era of renaissance has come out of new freedoms for peoples. The coming renaissance will be greater than any in human history, for this time all the peoples of the earth will share in it.

Pearl S. Buck, U.S. writer, 1892–1973 (in What America Means to Me, *1946)*

Sometime they'll give a war and nobody will come.
Carl Sandburg, U.S. writer and poet, 1878–1967 (in the poem "The People, Yes," 1936)

CLAUDIA DREIFUS: I read somewhere that you are predicting that the twenty-first century, unlike the twentieth, is to be a century of peace and justice. Why?

DALAI LAMA: Because I believe that in the twentieth century, humanity has learned from many, many experiences. Some positive, and many negative. What misery, what destruction! The greatest number of human beings were killed in the two world wars of this century. But human nature is such that when we face a tremendous critical situation, the human mind can wake up and find some other alternative. That is a human capacity.

Dalai Lama, contemporary Tibetan spiritual and temporal leader

LET US NOT ACCEPT VIOLENCE AS THE WAY TO PEACE.

Let us instead begin by respecting true freedom: The resulting peace will be able to satisfy the world's expectations; for it will be a peace built on justice, a peace founded on the incomparable dignity of the free human being.

John Paul II, contemporary Polish pope

The only thing we have to fear is fear itself.
Franklin D. Roosevelt, U.S. president, 1882–1945 (First Inaugural Address, March 4, 1933)

Be not afraid of life. Believe that life is worth living, and your belief will help create the fact.
William James, U.S. physician, psychologist and philosopher, 1842–1910

Some things have to be believed to be seen.
Ralph Hodgson, English poet, 1871–1962

We stand in witness to a planet-wide mutation of mind which promises to liberate energies of will and resources of vision long maturing in the depths of our identity.

Theodore Roszak, contemporary U.S. historian

A small body of determined spirits fired by an unquenchable faith in their mission can alter the course of history.

Mohandas K. Gandhi, Indian spiritual and nationalist leader, 1869–1948

THE START TO A BETTER WORLD
is the belief that it is possible.

Lily Tomlin, contemporary U.S. comedian and actor

Hope unbelieved is always considered nonsense. But hope believed is history in the process of being changed.

Jim Wallis, contemporary U.S. human rights activist, editor, and writer

Ah, the mysterious croak. Here today, gone tomorrow. It's the best reason I can think of to throw open the blinds and risk belief. Right now, this minute, time to move out into the grief and glory. High tide.

Barbara Kingsolver, contemporary U.S. writer (in High Tide in Tucson: Essays from Now or Never, *1996)*

It ain't over till it's over.

Yogi Berra, contemporary U.S. baseball player and manager

When fortune closes one door, it opens another.

Sa'di, Persian poet, 1213-1292

Where there's a will there's a way.

English Proverb

When you get to the end of your rope, tie a knot in it and hang on.

Eleanor Roosevelt, U.S. first lady and UN delegate, 1884–1962

He who endures to the end will be saved.

Jesus, Hebrew founder of Christianity, first century A.D.
(Matthew 10:22)

While there's life, there's hope.

Terence, Roman playwright, second century B.C.

Hope springs eternal in the human breast:
Man never is, but always to be blest.

Alexander Pope, English poet, 1688–1744

Hope begins in the dark, the stubborn hope that if you just show up and try to do the right thing, the dawn will come. You wait and watch and work: you don't give up.

Anne Lamott, contemporary U.S. writer (in Bird by Bird: Some Instructions on Writing and Life, *1995)*

12

MOST of the things worth doing in the world were said to be impossible before they were done.
Louis D. Brandeis, U.S. Supreme Court associate justice, 1856–1941

The difficult we do immediately.
The impossible takes a little longer.
U.S. Army Corps of Engineers, World War I motto

Throughout this toilsome world, alas!
Once and only once I pass;
If a kindness I may show,
If a good deed I may do
To a suffering fellow man,
Let me do it while I can.
No delay, for it is plain
I shall not pass this way again.

Anonymous ("I Shall Not Pass This Way Again")

I SAW a small girl walking up a hill carrying an infant boy on her shoulders and said to her, "This boy is too heavy for you." "Not at all," replied the girl, "he's my brother."

Anonymous

You will know the truth, and the truth will make you free.
Jesus, Hebrew founder of Christianity, first century A.D. (John 8:32)

The real advantage which truth has consists in this, that when an opinion is true, it may be extinguished once, twice, or many times, but in the course of ages there will generally be found persons to rediscover it, until some one of its reappearances falls on a time when from favorable circumstances it escapes persecution until it has made such head as to withstand all subsequent attempts to suppress it.

John Stuart Mill, English philosopher, 1806–1873

What has for centuries raised man above the beast is not the cudgel but an inward music: the irresistible power of unarmed truth, the powerful attraction of its example.

Boris Pasternak, Russian writer, 1890–1960
(in the novel Doctor Zhivago, *1957)*

TRULY DO I EXIST IN ALL BEINGS,

but I am most manifest in man. The human heart is my favorite dwelling place.

Srimad Bhagavatam, Hindu scriptures, fifth century B.C.

The place to improve the world is first in one's own heart and head and hands, and then work outward from there.

Robert M. Pirsig, contemporary U.S. writer (in Zen and the Art of Motorcycle Maintenance: An Inquiry into Values, *1974)*

In spite of everything I still believe that people are really good at heart.

Anne Frank, German-Jewish diarist and death-camp victim, 1929–1945

I SEE THE WORLD GRADUALLY being turned into a wilderness, I hear the ever approaching thunder, which will destroy us too. I can feel the sufferings of millions and yet, if I look up into the heavens, I think that it will all come right, that this cruelty too will end, and that peace and tranquility will return again.

In the meantime, I must uphold my ideals, for perhaps the time will come when I shall be able to carry them out.

Anne Frank, German-Jewish diarist and death-camp victim, 1929–1945

THEN I WAS STANDING ON THE HIGHEST MOUNTAIN OF THEM ALL.

. . . And I saw that the sacred hoop of my people was one of many hoops that made one circle, wide as daylight and as starlight, and in the center grew one mighty flowering tree to shelter all the children of one mother and one father. And I saw that it was holy.

Black Elk, Native American chief, 1862–1950

20

IN the depth of winter, I finally learned that within me there lay an invincible summer.
Albert Camus, French writer, 1913–1960

Our Father-Mother God, all-harmonious.
Mary Baker Eddy, U.S. founder of the Christian Science Church,
1821–1910

*I*f today's planetary civilization has any hope of survival, that hope lies chiefly in what we understand as the human spirit.

Václav Havel, contemporary Czech president

None of us knows all the potentialities that slumber in the spirit of the population, or all the ways in which that population can surprise us when there is the right interplay of events.

Václav Havel, contemporary Czech president

I BELIEVE WE SHALL in some manner be cherished by our Maker—that the One who gave us this remarkable earth has the power still farther to surprise that which He has caused. Beyond that all is silence.

Emily Dickinson, U.S. poet, 1830–1886

I think it not improbable that man, like the grub that prepares a chamber for the winged thing it never has seen but is to be—that man may have cosmic destinies that he does not understand. And so beyond the vision of battling races and an impoverished earth, I catch a dreaming glimpse of peace.

Oliver Wendell Holmes Jr., U.S. Supreme Court chief justice, 1841–1935

24

MAN IN THIS MOMENT of his history has emerged in greater supremacy over the forces of nature than has ever been dreamed of before. He has it in his power to solve quite easily the problems of material existence. He has conquered the wild beasts, and he has even conquered the insect and microbes. There lies before him, as he wishes, a golden age of peace and progress. All is in his hand. He has only to conquer his last and worst enemy—himself. With vision, faith and courage, it may be within our power to win a crowning victory for all.

Winston Churchill, British prime minister, 1874–1965(1950)

Is there a spiritual reality,

inconceivable to us today, which corresponds in history to the physical reality which Einstein discovered and which led to the atomic bomb? Einstein discovered a law of physical change: the way to convert a single particle of matter into enormous physical energy. Might there not also be, as Gandhi suggested, an equally incredible and [as yet] undiscovered law of spiritual change, whereby a single person or small community of persons could be converted into an enormous spiritual energy capable of transforming a society and a world?

James W. Douglass, contemporary U.S. human rights activist and writer (in Lightning East to West*, 1980)*

We shall not cease from exploration
And the end of all our exploring
Will be to arrive where we started
And know the place for the first time.

T. S. Eliot, U.S.-born English poet, 1888–
1965 (in the poem "Little Gidding," 1943)

In the infinite distances
there must be a place
there must be a place
where all is light
and that the light from that high place
where all is light
simply hasn't got here yet.

*Lawrence Ferlinghetti, contemporary U.S.
poet (in the poem "Olbers' Paradox")*

THE HUMAN CONDITION is something at once
horrible and marvelous. We are very badly made, but we are not finished.
Eduardo Galeano, contemporary Uruguayan writer

No human being is so bad as to be beyond redemption.
*Mohandas K. Gandhi, Indian spiritual and nationalist leader,
1869–1948*

Have patience, Candidate, as one who fears no failure, courts no success. Fix thy Soul's gaze upon the star whose ray thou art.
The Book of the Golden Precepts, *ancient Buddhist writing*

What is more glorious than a soul when it liberates itself?

André Gide, French writer, 1869–1951

Act well your part, there all the honor lies.

Alexander Pope, English poet, 1688–1744

Our greatest glory consists not in never falling, but in rising every time we fall.

Oliver Goldsmith, English writer, 1730–1774

$\mathcal{S}$ATISFACTION lies in the effort, not in the attainment. Full effort is full victory.

Mohandas K. Gandhi, Indian spiritual and nationalist leader, 1869–1948

There is no failure except in no longer trying.

Elbert Hubbard, U.S. writer, editor, and humorist, 1856–1915

WHEN THE MORNING'S FRESHNESS

has been replaced by the weariness of midday, when the leg muscles quiver under the strain, the climb seems endless, and, suddenly, nothing will go quite as you wish—it is then that you must not hesitate.

Dag Hammarskjöld, Swedish statesman and UN secretary general, 1905–1961 (in Markings, *1964)*

When the one Great Scorer comes
To write against your name,
He marks—not that you won or lost—
But how you played the game.

Grantland Rice, U.S. journalist, 1880–1954
(in the poem "Alumnus Football," 1925)

Forget not that the earth delights to feel your bare feet and the winds long to play with your hair.

Kahlil Gibran, Syrian poet, 1883–1931

Never cease to be convinced that life might be better—your own and that of others; not a future life that might console us for the present one and help us to accept its misery, but this one of ours.

André Gide, French writer, 1869–1951

THE RADIANCE IN SOME PLACES

is so great as to be fairly dazzling, keen lance rays of every color flashing, sparkling in glorious abundance, joining the plants in their fine, brave beauty-work—every crystal, every flower a window opening into heaven, a mirror reflecting the Creator.

John Muir, Scottish-born U.S. naturalist, 1838–1914

All are but parts of
one stupendous whole,
Whose body Nature is,
and God the soul.

*Alexander Pope, English
poet, 1688–1744 (in the poem
"An Essay on Man," 1734)*

We shall overcome, we shall overcome,
We shall overcome some day.
Oh, deep in my heart I do believe,
We shall overcome some day.

Anonymous (in the civil rights song "We Shall Overcome," 1946)

[The] TRANSFORMATION OF MAN

into an active, responsible individual is the new event which, more than any other, characterizes man. Of course the ancient mechanism of evolution, natural selection, will again enter into play. But, instead of depending as formerly on the slow action of biological laws and of chance, natural selection now depends on conscience, a manifestation of cerebral activity based on freedom which becomes, in each of us, the means put at our disposal to advance.

Pierre Lecomte du Noüy, French biologist, 1883-1947

The glory of human nature lies in our seeming capacity to exercise conscious control of our own destiny.

Winston Churchill, British prime minister, 1874–1965

*N*o problem of human destiny
is beyond human beings.

John F. Kennedy, U.S. president, 1917–1963

THE HUMAN SPECIES CAN, if it wishes, transcend itself—not just sporadically, an individual here in one way, an individual there in another way, but in its entirety, as humanity…The human species [is] on the threshold of a new kind of existence, as different from ours as ours is from that of Peking man. It will at last be consciously fulfilling its real destiny.

Julian Huxley, English biologist, 1887–1975

MAN'S RESPONSIBILITY AND DESTINY

[is] to be an agent for the rest of the world in the job of realizing its inherent potentialities as fully as possible. It is as if man had been suddenly appointed managing director of the biggest business of all, the business of evolution...Whether he is conscious of what he is doing or not, he is in point of fact determining the future direction of evolution on this earth.

Julian Huxley, English biologist, 1887–1975

43

IT IS POSSIBLE TO BELIEVE that all the past is but the beginning of a beginning, and that all that is and has been is but the twilight of the dawn. It is possible to believe that all that the human mind has ever accomplished is but the dream before the awakening … All this world is heavy with the promise of greater things, and a day will come in the unending succession of days when beings, beings who are now latent in our thoughts and hidden in our loins shall stand upon this earth as one stands upon a footstool, and shall laugh and reach out their hands amid the stars.

H. G. Wells, English writer, 1866–1946(1902)

I THINK THAT THE HUMAN RACE

does command its own destiny and that that destiny can eventually embrace the stars.

Lorraine Hansberry, U.S. writer, 1930–1965

MARILYN MONROE: How do you find your way back in the dark?
CLARK GABLE: Just head for that big star straight on. The highway's under it. It'll take us right home.

Arthur Miller, contemporary U.S. playwright
(in the film The Misfits, *1961)*

PA JOAD: We sure are takin' abeatin'.

MA JOAD: I know. That's what make us tough. Rich fellas come up an' th' die an' their kids ain't no good, and they die out, but we keep acomin'. We're the people that live. They can't wipe us out. They can't lick us. We'll go on forever, pa, 'cause we're the people.

John Steinbeck, U.S. writer, 1902–1968
(in the film Grapes of Wrath, *1940)*

THE GREATEST TEST OF COURAGE IS TO BEAR DEFEAT WITHOUT LOSING HEART.

Robert G. Ingersoll, U.S. lawyer and lecturer, 1833–1899

Not in the clamor of the crowded
street,
Not in the shouts and plaudits of
the throng,
But in ourselves, are triumph and
defeat.

Henry Wadsworth Longfellow, U.S. poet,
1807–1882 (in the poem "The Poets," 1876)

What does not kill me makes me stronger.

Friedrich Nietzsche, German philosopher, 1844–1900
(in Twilight of the Idols, 1889)

Man is not made for defeat.
A man can be destroyed but not defeated.

Ernest Hemingway, U.S. writer, 1899–1961
(in The Old Man and the Sea, *1952)*

IF I am not for myself, who is for me? And when I am for myself only, what am I? And if not now, when?

Hillel, Hebrew teacher, first century B.C.

It is better to die on your feet than to live on your knees!

Dolores Ibárruri (known as La Pasionaria), Spanish journalist and revolutionary leader, 1895–1989

THESE ARE THE TIMES THAT TRY MEN'S SOULS.

The summer soldier and the sunshine patriot will, in this crisis, shrink from the service of his country; but he that stands it now, deserves the love and thanks of man and woman. Tyranny, like hell, is not easily conquered; yet we have this consolation with us, that the harder the conflict, the more glorious the triumph. What we obtain too cheap, we esteem too lightly: 'Tis dearness only that gives every thing its value. Heaven knows how to put a proper price upon its goods; and it would be strange indeed, if so celestial an article as FREEDOM should not be highly rated.

Thomas Paine, English-born U.S. political philosopher, 1737–1809
(in The Crisis, *1776)*

I'm mad as hell, and I'm not going to take it anymore.

Paddy Chayefsky, U.S. playwright, 1923–1981
(in the film Network, *1976)*

*T*here are circumstances which have to do with simple human honor. No matter the risk. To resist and not surrender.

Antonin Artaud, French playwright, 1896–1948

Is life so dear or peace so sweet, as to be purchased at the price of chains and slavery? **FORBID IT, ALMIGHTY GOD!** I know not what course others may take, but as for me, give me liberty or give me death!

Patrick Henry, U.S. revolutionary leader, 1736–1799(1775)

We hold these truths to be self-evident, that all men are created equal, that they are endowed by their Creator with certain unalienable rights, that among these are *life, liberty, and the pursuit of happiness.*

Thomas Jefferson, U.S. president, 1743–1826 (Declaration of Independence, 1776)

WE HOLD THESE TRUTHS TO BE SELF-EVIDENT: that all men and women are created equal; that they are endowed by their Creator with certain alienable rights; that among these are life, liberty, and the pursuit of happiness.

Elizabeth Cady Stanton, U.S. women's rights leader and writer, 1815–1892 (Declaration of Sentiments, 1848)

Congress shall make no law respecting an establishment of religion, or prohibiting the free exercise thereof; or abridging the freedom of speech or of the press; or the right of the people peaceably to assemble; and petition the government for a redress of grievances.

Constitution of the United States (Bill of Rights, First Amendment, 1791)

*A*nd so, my fellow Americans: ask not what your country can do for you— ask what you can do for your country. My fellow citizens of the world: ask not what America will do for you, but what together we can do for the freedom of man.

John F. Kennedy, U.S. president, 1917–1963

Never before has man had such capacity to control his own environment, to end thirst and hunger, to conquer poverty and disease, to banish illiteracy and massive human misery. We have the power to make this the best generation of mankind in the history of the world—or to make it the last.

John F. Kennedy, U.S. president, 1917–1963

Every crisis has both its dangers and its opportunities. Each can spell either salvation or doom. In a dark, confused world the spirit of God may yet reign supreme.

Martin Luther King Jr., U.S. clergyman and human rights leader, 1929–1968 (in Stride Toward Freedom, *1958)*

We here highly resolve that these dead shall not have died in vain—that this nation, under God, shall have a new birth of freedom—and that government of the people, by the people, for the people, *shall not perish from the earth.*

Abraham Lincoln, U.S. president, 1809–1865 (in Gettysburg Address, 1863)

58

WITH MALICE TOWARD NONE; with charity for all; with firmness in the right, as God gives us to see the right, let us strive on to finish the work we are in; to bind up the nation's wounds; to care for him who shall have borne the battle, and for his widow, and his orphan—to do all which may achieve and cherish a just, and a lasting peace, among ourselves, and with all nations.

Abraham Lincoln, U.S. president, 1809–1865 (Second Inaugural Address, March 4, 1865)

THE eternal mystery of the world is its comprehensibility.

Albert Einstein, German-born U.S. physicist, 1879–1955

Beyond all mystery is the mercy of God.

Abraham Joshua Heschel, German-born U.S. theologian, 1907–1972

In every age I come back
To deliver the holy,
To destroy the sin of the sinner,
To establish righteousness.

Bhagavad Gita, Hindu scriptures,
sixth century B.C.

Thou dost show me
the path of life
in thy presence there is
fullness of joy.

Bible (Psalms 16:11)

Fear not, for I am with you,
be not dismayed, for I am your God;
I will strengthen you, I will help you,
I will uphold you with my victorious
right hand.

Isaiah, Hebrew prophet,
eighth century B.C. (Isaiah 41:10)

The wolf shall dwell with the lamb,
and the leopard shall lie down
with the kid,
and the calf and the lion
and the fatling together,
and a little child shall lead them...
They shall not hurt or destroy
in all my holy mountain;
for the earth shall be full of
the knowledge of the Lord
as the waters cover the sea.

*Isaiah, Hebrew prophet,
eighth century B.C. (Isaiah 11:6–9)*

You shall go out in joy,
and be led forth in peace;
the mountains and the hills before you
shall break forth into singing,
and the trees of the field
shall clap their hands.

Isaiah, Hebrew prophet,
eighth century B.C. (Isaiah 55:12)

They shall build houses and inhabit them;
they shall plant vineyards and eat their fruit.
They shall not build and another inhabit;
they shall not plant and another eat.

Isaiah, Hebrew prophet,
eighth century B.C. (Isaiah 65:21–22)

They shall beat their swords into plowshares,
and their spears into pruning hooks;
nation shall not lift up sword against nation,
neither shall they learn war any more;
but they shall sit every man under his vine
and under his fig tree,
and none shall make them afraid;
for the mouth of the Lord of hosts has
spoken.

Micah, Hebrew prophet,
eighth century B.C. (Micah 4:3–4)

THE KINGDOM OF HEAVEN IS LIKE

a grain of mustard seed which a man took and sowed in his field; it is the smallest of all seeds, but when it has grown it is the greatest of shrubs and becomes a tree, so that the birds of the air come and make nests in its branches.

Jesus, Hebrew founder of Christianity, first century A.D.
(Matthew 13:31–32)

I HEARD A GREAT VOICE from the throne saying, "Behold, the dwelling of God is with men. He will dwell with them, and they shall be his people, and God himself will be with them; he will wipe away every tear from their eyes, and death shall be no more, neither shall there be mourning nor crying nor pain any more, for the former things have passed away." And he who sat upon the throne said, *"Behold, I make all things new."*

John, Christian apostle, first century A.D. (Revelations 21:3–5)

$\mathcal{D}$ISCOURAGED not by difficulties without, or the anguish of ages within, the heart listens to a secret voice that whispers: "Be not dismayed; in the future lies the Promised Land."

Helen Keller, U.S. writer and lecturer, 1880–1968

The Promised Land always lies on the other side of a wilderness.

Havelock Ellis, English physician and psychologist, 1859–1939

The Lord is my shepherd, I shall not want;
He makes me lie down in green pastures.
He leads me beside still waters;
He restores my soul.
He leads me in paths of righteousness
for His name's sake.
Even though I walk through the valley
of the shadow of death,
I fear no evil;
for Thou art with me;
Thy rod and Thy staff,
they comfort me.

Bible (Psalms 23:1–4)

Our Father who art in heaven,
Hallowed be Thy name.
Thy kingdom come,
Thy will be done,
On earth as it is in heaven.
Give us this day our daily bread;
And forgive us our debts,
As we also have forgiven our debtors;
And lead us not into temptation,
But deliver us from evil.

Jesus, Hebrew founder of Christianity,
first century A.D. (Matthew 6:9–13)

O divine Master, grant that I may not
so much seek
To be consoled as to console;
To be understood as to understand;
To be loved as to love.
For it is in giving that we receive;
It is in pardoning that we are pardoned;
And it is in dying that we are born to
eternal life.

*St. Francis of Assisi, Italian religious leader,
1181?–1226 (in "The Prayer of St. Francis")*

To forgive wrongs darker than death or night;
To defy Power, which seems omnipotent;
To love, and bear; to hope till Hope creates
From its own wreck the thing it contemplates.

Percy Bysshe Shelley, English poet, 1792–1822 (in the poem "Prometheus Unbound," 1820)

We forgive to the extent we love.

François de La Rochefoucauld, French writer, 1613–1680

THE DAILY BREAD OF GRACE, WITHOUT WHICH NOTHING CAN BE ACHIEVED, IS GIVEN TO THE EXTENT TO WHICH WE OURSELVES GIVE AND FORGIVE.

Aldous Huxley, English writer, 1894–1963

God, give us grace to accept with serenity the things which cannot be changed, courage to change the things which should be changed, and *the wisdom to distinguish the one from the other.*

Reinhold Niebuhr, U.S. theologian, 1892–1971 (attributed)

GOD works by contraries so that a man feels himself to be lost in the very moment when he is on the point of being saved.

Martin Luther, German founder of Protestantism, 1483–1546

It is only at the gates of hell that salvation looms.

Henry Miller, U.S. writer, 1891–1980

THREE WORDS WERE IN THE CAPTAIN'S HEART. He shaped them soundlessly with his trembling lips, as he had not breath to spare for a whisper, *"I am lost."* And having given up life, the captain suddenly began to live.

Carson McCullers (Lulu Carson Smith McCullers), U.S. writer, 1917–1967 (in the novel Reflections in a Golden Eye, *1941)*

*A*T the moment you are most in awe of all there is about life that you don't understand, you are closer to understanding it all than at any other time.

Jane Wagner, contemporary U.S. writer and humorist

There will come a time when you believe everything is finished. That will be the beginning.

Louis L'Amour, U.S. writer, 1908–1988 (in the novel Lonely on the Mountain, *1980)*

***Ubuntu* IS VERY DIFFICULT** to render into a Western language. It speaks of the very essence of being human. When we want to give high praise to someone we say, "Yu u nobuntu"; "Hey, so-and-so has ubuntu." Then you are generous, you are hospitable, you are friendly and caring and compassionate. You share what you have. It is to say, "My humanity is caught up, is inextricably bound up, in yours." We belong in a bundle of life. We say, "A person is a person through other persons." It is not, "I think therefore I am." It says rather: **"I AM HUMAN BECAUSE I BELONG. I PARTICIPATE, I SHARE."**

Desmond Tutu, contemporary South African bishop and human rights leader

80

COURAGE, MY FRIENDS, 'TIS NOT TOO LATE TO MAKE A BETTER WORLD.

Thomas Clement "Tommy" Douglass, Canadian clergyman and political leader, 1904-1986

Not enjoyment, and not sorrow,
Is our destined end or way;
But to act, that each tomorrow
Find us farther than today.

Henry Wadsworth Longfellow,
U.S. poet, 1807–1882 (in the poem
"A Psalm of Life," 1839)

What progress, you
ask, have I made?
I have begun to be
a friend to myself.

*Hecato, Greek philosopher,
third century B.C.*

I am in the world
to change the world.

Muriel Rukreyser,
U.S. poet and writer, 1913–1980
(in the poem "Women As Market," 1968)

*N*ever doubt that a small group of thoughtful, committed citizens can change the world; indeed, it's the only thing that ever has.

Margaret Mead, U.S. anthropologist, 1901–1978 (attributed)

*T*HERE is no obstacle which cannot be broken down by wills sufficiently keyed up, if they deal with it in time. There is thus no inescapable historic law.

Henri Bergson, French philosopher, 1859–1941

Human beings, by changing the inner attitudes of their minds can change the outer aspects of their lives.

William James, U.S. physician, psychologist, and philosopher, 1842–1910

THE SEARCH IS WHAT ANYONE WOULD UNDERTAKE if he were not sunk in the everydayness of his own life. . . . To become aware of the possibility of the search is to be onto something. Not to be onto something is to be in despair.

Walker Percy, U.S. writer, 1916–1990 (in the novel The Moviegoer, *1961)*

I read and walked for miles at night along the beach, writing bad blank verse and searching endlessly for someone wonderful who would step out of the darkness and change my life. *It never crossed my mind that that person could be me.*

Anna Quindlen, contemporary U.S. journalist

Our discontent begins by finding false villains whom we can accuse of deceiving us. Next we find false heroes whom we expect to liberate us. The hardest, most discomfiting discovery is that each of us must emancipate himself.

Daniel J. Boorstin, contemporary U.S. historian (in The Image: A Guide to Pseudo-Events in America, *1961)*

THE WORLD IS GOD'S SUFFERING,

and every individual human being who wishes even to approach his own wholeness knows very well that this means bearing his own cross. But the eternal promise for him who bears his own cross is the Paraclete.

Carl G. Jung, Swiss psychiatrist and founder of analytical psychology, 1875–1961

The more we realize our minuteness and our impotence in the face of cosmic forces, the more amazing becomes what human beings have achieved.

Bertrand Russell, English mathematician and philosopher, 1872–1970

Man, unlike any other thing organic or inorganic in the universe, grows beyond his work, walks up the stairs of his concepts, emerges ahead of his accomplishments.

John Steinbeck, U.S. writer, 1902–1968
(in the novel Grapes of Wrath, *1939)*

Life is about becoming more than we are.
Oprah Winfrey, contemporary U.S. television talk-show host

The important thing is this: to be able at any moment to sacrifice what we are for what we could become.
Charles Du Bos, French critic, 1882–1939

No one can make you feel inferior without your consent.
Eleanor Roosevelt, U.S. first lady and UN delegate, 1884–1962

The development of the individual can be described as a succession of new births at consecutively higher levels.

Maria Montessori, Italian physician and educator, 1870–1952

NEVER BEND YOUR HEAD! ALWAYS HOLD IT HIGH! LOOK THE WORLD STRAIGHT IN THE FACE!

Helen Keller, U.S. writer and lecturer, 1880–1968

Walk tall as the trees; live strong as the mountains; be gentle as the spring winds; keep the warmth of summer in your heart, and the Great Spirit will always be with you.

Native American chant, nineteenth century

Be strong and of good courage, do not fear or be in dread of them: for it is the Lord your God who goes with you; He will not fail you or forsake you.

Moses, Hebrew founder of Judaism, fourteenth century B.C.
(Deuteronomy 31:6)

*L*ife is not meant to be easy, my child;
but take courage: it can be delightful.

*George Bernard Shaw, British playwright and critic, 1856–1950
(in the play* Back to Methuselah, *1921)*

THERE IS NO REASON WHY, in the ages to come, the sort of man who is now exceptional should not become usual, and if that were to happen, the exceptional man in that new world would rise as far above Shakespeare as Shakespeare now rises above the common man.

Bertrand Russell, English mathematician and philosopher,
1872–1970 (in Human Society in Ethics and Politics, *1962)*

THE TURNING POINT in the process of growing up

is when you discover the core of strength within you that survives all hurt.

Max Lerner, U.S. writer, 1902–1992

It's not what they take away from you that counts: *it's what you do with what you have left.*

Hubert H. Humphrey, Minnesota senator and U.S. vice president, 1911–1978

We only become what we are by the radical and deep-seated refusal of that which others have made of us.

Jean-Paul Sartre, French philosopher, 1905–1980

CHARACTER is what emerges from all the little things you were too busy to do yesterday, but did anyway.

Mignon McLaughlin, contemporary U.S. writer

This above all: to thine own self be true,
And it must follow, as the night the day,
Thou canst not then be false to any man.

William Shakespeare, English playwright, 1564–1616
(in the play Hamlet, 1600)

NO MAN IS AN ISLAND, ENTIRE OF ITSELF; every man is a piece of the Continent, a part of the main; if a clod be washed away by the sea, Europe is the less, as well as if a promontory were, as well as if a manor of thy friends or of thine own were; any man's death diminishes me because I am involved in Mankind; And therefore never send to know for whom the bell tolls; it tolls for thee.

John Donne, English poet, 1572–1631
(in Devotions Upon Emergent Occasions, 1624)

99

If I can stop one Heart from breaking
I shall not live in vain.
If I can ease one Life the Aching
Or cool one Pain
Or help one fainting Robin
Unto his Nest again
I shall not live in Vain.

Emily Dickinson, U.S. poet, 1830–1886

WE are members one of another; so that you cannot injure or help your neighbor without injuring or helping yourself.

George Bernard Shaw, British playwright and critic, 1856–1950 (in the play Androcles and the Lion, *1912)*

Remember, nobody wins unless everybody wins.

Bruce Springsteen, contemporary U.S. songwriter and singer

IF LIFE IS TO BE FULLY HUMAN

it must serve some end which seems, in some sense, outside human life, some end which is impersonal and above mankind, such as God or truth or beauty. Those who best promote life do not have life for their purpose. They aim rather at what seems like a gradual incarnation, a bringing into our human existence of something eternal, something that appears to imagination to live in a heaven remote from strife and failure and the devouring jaws of Time.

Bertrand Russell, English mathematician and philosopher, 1872–1970 (in Principles of Social Reconstruction, *1916)*

102

THIS IS THE TRUE JOY IN LIFE,

the being used for a purpose recognized by yourself as a mighty one; the being thoroughly worn out before you are thrown on the scrap heap; the being a force of Nature instead of a feverish, selfish, little clod of ailments and grievances complaining that the world will not devote itself to making you happy.

George Bernard Shaw, British playwright and critic, 1856–1950 (in the play Man and Superman, *1903)*

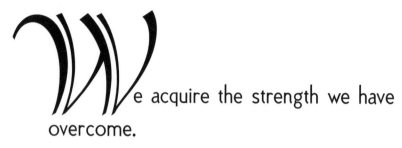

We acquire the strength we have overcome.

Ralph Waldo Emerson, U.S. philosopher, 1803–1882
(in the essay "Considerations by the Way," 1860)

Strength is granted to us all when we are needed to serve great causes.

Winston Churchill, British prime minister, 1874–1965

THE FRUIT OF THE SPIRIT IS love, joy, peace, patience, kindness, goodness, faithfulness, gentleness, self-control; against such there is no law.

Paul, Christian apostle, first century A.D. (Galatians 5:22–23)

Whenever we do what we can, *we immediately can do more.*

James Freeman Clarke, U.S. clergyman, 1810–1888

*B*E ashamed to die until you have won some victory for humanity.

Horace Mann, U.S. educator, 1796–1859

Kindness is the mark of faith; and whoever has not kindness has not faith.

Muhammad, Arab founder of Islam, A.D. 570–632

THE STRUGGLE WHICH IS NOT JOYOUS IS THE WRONG STRUGGLE. The joy of the struggle is not hedonism and hilarity, but the sense of purpose, achievement and dignity.

Germaine Greer, contemporary Australian writer
(in The Female Eunuch, *1970)*

FOR MOST HUMAN BEINGS, life, when reduced to its essence, is a never-ending search for respect. First and most important, self-respect, then the respect of others. There are many ways to achieve respect but none more certain and rewarding than in service to others ... What you will find is that fulfillment in life will come, not from acquiring things, not from leisure, not from self-indulgence. Real fulfillment in your life will come from striving with all of your physical and spiritual might for a worthwhile objective that helps others and is larger than your self-interest.

George J. Mitchell, contemporary Maine senator
(commencement address, 2003)

There is no fear in love, but perfect love casts out fear.

John, Christian apostle, first century A.D. (1 John 4:18)

*T*here is only one happiness in life,
to love and be loved.

George Sand (Armandine-Aurore-Lucile Dudevant),
French writer, 1804–1876

CALL the world, if you please, "The vale of Soul-making."

John Keats, English poet, 1795–1821

A fella ain't got a soul of his own, but on'y a piece of a big one.

John Steinbeck, U.S. writer, 1902–1968 (in the novel Grapes of Wrath, *1939)*

I THINK US HERE TO WONDER, MYSELF. To wonder. To ast. And that in wondering bout the big things and asting bout the big things, you learn about the little ones, almost by accident. But you never know nothing more about the big things than you start out with. The more I wonder, he say, the more I love.

And people start to love you back, I bet, I say.

They do, he say, surprise.

Alice Walker, contemporary U.S. writer
(in the novel The Color Purple, *1982)*

LIFE IS SO PRECIOUS. Please, please, let's love one another, live each day, reach out to each other, be kind to each other. Peace be with you. God is great.

Julia Roberts, contemporary U.S. actor (closing words of her presentation at a nationally televised benefit for the September 11th victims and their families, September 21, 2001)

If mankind is to escape its programmed self-extinction the God who saves us will not descend from the machine: *He will rise up again in the human soul.*

Lewis Mumford, U.S. sociologist, 1895–1990 (in The Pentagon of Power: The Myth of the Machine, *1970)*

ONE OF TWO THINGS MUST HAPPEN. Either out of that darkness some new creation will come to supplant us as we have supplanted the animals, or the heavens will fall in thunder and destroy us.

George Bernard Shaw, British playwright and critic, 1856–1950

You see things; and you say, "Why?" But I dream things that never were; and I say, "Why not?"

George Bernard Shaw, British playwright and critic, 1856–1950 (in the play Back to Methuselah, 1921)

I believe that man will not merely endure: he will prevail. He is immortal, not because he alone among creatures has an inexhaustible voice, but because he has a soul, a spirit capable of compassion and sacrifice and endurance.

William Faulkner, U.S. writer, 1897–1962

THE HUMAN SOUL, THE WORLD,

the universe are laboring on to their magnificent consummation. We are not fashioned marvelously for nought.

Ralph Waldo Emerson, U.S. philosopher, 1803–1882

118

WE ARE NOW MOVING INTO a chapter of human history in which our choice is going to be, not between a whole world and a shredded-up world, but between one world and no world. I believe that the human race is going to choose life and good, not death and evil. I therefore believe in the imminence of one world, and I believe that, in the twenty-first century, human life is going to be a unity again in all its aspects and activities.

Arnold J. Toynbee, English historian, 1889–1975 (in the essay "It Is, 'One World or No World,'" 1964)

Things fall apart; the center cannot hold;
Mere anarchy is loosed upon the world,
The blood-dimmed tide is loosed, and everywhere
The ceremony of innocence is drowned;
The best lack all conviction, while the worst
Are full of passionate intensity.
Surely some revelation is at hand;
Surely the Second Coming is at hand.

William Butler Yeats, Irish poet, 1865–1939
(in the poem "The Second Coming," 1921)

I SAY, "YOU ARE GODS,
SONS OF THE MOST HIGH, ALL OF YOU."

Bible (Psalms 82:6)

[MANKIND HAS THE RESPONSIBILITY] for deciding if they want merely to live, or intend to make just the extra effort required for fulfilling, even on this refractory planet, the essential function of the universe, which is a machine for the making of gods.

Henri Bergson, French philosopher, 1859–1941 (in The Two Sources of Morality and Religion, *1932)*

121

If there is a God, we're all it.

John Lennon, English songwriter and singer, 1940–1980

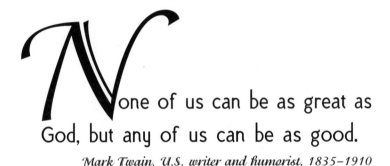

None of us can be as great as God, but any of us can be as good.

Mark Twain, U.S. writer and humorist, 1835–1910

I AM THOU, AND THOU ART I; and wheresoever thou mayest be I am there. In all am I scattered, and whensoever thou willest, thou gatherest Me; and gathering Me, thou gatherest Thyself.

Gospel of Eve, Christian writing, fourth century A.D.

I FIND THE GREAT THING IN THIS

world is not so much where we stand, as in what direction we are moving. To reach the port of heaven, we must sail sometimes with the wind and sometimes against it—but we must sail, and not drift, nor lie at anchor.

Oliver Wendell Holmes Sr., U.S. physician and writer, 1809–1894

Sail forth—steer for the deep waters only,
Reckless O soul, exploring, I with thee, and thou with me,
For we are bound where mariner has not yet dared to go,
And we will risk the ship, ourselves and all.
O my brave soul!
O farther farther sail!
O daring joy, but safe! are they not all the seas of God?
O farther, farther, farther sail!

*Walt Whitman, U.S. poet, 1819–1891 (in the poem
"Passage to India," 1871)*

LOVE THE EARTH AND SUN AND THE ANIMALS, DESPISE RICHES...devote your income and labor to others, hate tyrants, argue not concerning God, have patience and indulgence toward the people, take off your hat to nothing known or unknown...re-examine all you have been told at school or church or in any book, dismiss whatever insults your own soul, and your very flesh shall be a great poem.

Walt Whitman, U.S. poet, 1819–1891 (in "Leaves of Grass," 1855)

Traveler, there are no paths; paths are made by walking.

Spanish Proverb

A journey of a thousand miles begins with a single step.

Chinese Proverb

It's a long road that has no turning.

English Proverb

THE road before us is shorter than the road behind.

Lucy Stone, editor and U.S. women rights leader, 1818–1893

When your cart reaches the foot of the mountain, a path will appear.

Chinese Proverb

IT is better to light a candle than curse the darkness.
Chinese Proverb

Darkness heralds light.
English Proverb

THERE IS A POWER NOW SLUMBERING WITHIN US, WHICH IF AWAKENED WOULD DO TO EVIL WHAT LIGHT DOES TO DARKNESS.

Mohandas K. Gandhi, Indian spiritual and nationalist leader,
1869–1948

Remember the feeling as a child
when you woke up and morning smiled,
it's time you felt like that again.

Taj Mahal, contemporary U.S.
songwriter and singer (in the song
"Take a Giant Step," 1969)

NATHANIEL HAWTHORNE: Are you a good little boy?

JULIAN (HIS THREE-YEAR-OLD SON): Yes.

NATHANIEL: Why are you good?

JULIAN: Because I love all people.

Julian Hawthorne, son of U.S. writer
Nathaniel Hawthorne, 1804–1864
(the latter's diary entry September 6, 1849)

Lo, soul, seest thou not God's purpose
from the first?
The earth to be spann'd, connected by
network,
The races, neighbors, to marry and be
given in marriage,
The ocean to be cross'd, the distant
brought near,
The lands to be welded together.

*Walt Whitman, U.S. poet, 1819–1891
(in the poem "Passage to India," 1871)*

134

Man is of soul and body, formed for deeds
Of high resolve, on fancy's boldest wing
To soar unwearied.

Percy Bysshe Shelley, English poet, 1792–1822
(in the poem "Queen Mab," 1813)

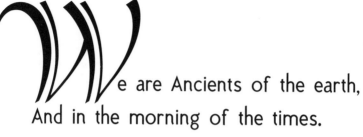

We are Ancients of the earth,
And in the morning of the times.

Alfred, Lord Tennyson, English poet, 1809–1892
(in the poem "The Day Dream," 1842)

The strongest and sweetest songs
yet remain to be sung.

Walt Whitman, U.S. poet, 1819–1891

Read all three books in the series:

Inspiring Quotes

Love Quotes

Money Quotes